The People We Meet Along The Way

Krystle Havenar

BookLeaf Publishing

India | USA | UK

Made with ❤ on the BookLeaf Publishing Platform
www.bookleafpub.in
www.bookleafpub.com

Dedication

To Sara, Celisse, Amber, and all the creatives.

Preface

The people we meet can have a profound impact on us, in both positive and negative ways. They can give us examples of how to be our best selves possible and also show us the type of person we don't want to be. This collection was inspired by just that-- people, and the lasting impacts they have on others. I hope you all are able to take something away from this and enjoy reading each poem as much as I enjoyed writing them.

Acknowledgements

Over the years, I have been instructed, impacted, and inspired by so many people. If I were to name everyone that has helped me grow as a poet, I would never have enough space, so instead I've chosen a few that were the most impactful. Firstly, I would like to thank Prof. Hope Coulter. You not only taught me so much about writing poetry and finding my own style, but also encouraged me to continue writing and developing my skills and creativity. I would also like to thank my husband, Zac, for helping push me out of my poetry journals and into the world of print. So many of my friends have been pivotal in this journey, but I will only name a few here: Kelli, Cecilia, and Kelsey, thank you for everything you did to help me refine, grow, and stretch my creativity. Lastly, thank you, all the readers, who have purchased this book and helped make me successful. With so much gratitude in my heart, thank you all.

Momma

She was raised by the salt of the earth;
two pillars of strength
that held up her entire world.
They met all her needs each day
and also the needs of each of her four siblings,
all while they managed their farm
and store.
She spent a good portion of her childhood in the wheat
fields,
with silos to provide overwatch
and barn cats to keep her safe.
And she also spent time in the tailoring store,
with clothes pins to keep her on the right track
and thread to keep her from unraveling.
She was raised to work hard for her family,
but also to have fun;
she grew up in the era of bottle-rocket fights,
went to a high school that valued football above all else,
and never had to lock her house door at night.

She was taught to be a fighter,
that the battle wasn't over until the last bottle-rocket
was launched.
She learned to be strategic,

calculated what she had
and used it to get what she wanted.
"No" never meant giving up to her;
it was just a new challenge to overcome.
She was fierce in every way—
she was tough as any of the boys,
yet graceful;
no matter what job she found for herself,
she held her head high and worked hard
until she could come home,
unpin her bleached blonde curls so they were as wild
and free as her soul,
and make memories with me and my brother.
She would play games and read us stories
until the day was over and we were safely tucked
into our beds.

She never shied away from who she was.
She taught me how to be a lady,
but also how to stand up for myself.
She passed down her own childhood lessons,
taught me all about embroidery, how to measure
inseams,
how to iron and starch our clothes to perfection.
She taught me how to garden
as we raked leaves side by side,
talked to me about fertilizers, weeding, and pruning.

She gardened with love and respect,
taught me the value of the plants that feed us and
decorate this world.

She left pieces of herself in me.
She's returned to the earth from which she was grown,
but she still lives on in this world.
I know each time I'm working in the garden
or threading a needle,
her hands guide mine
and her strength is behind me
as I navigate new challenges.

I know this for certain
because I can still hear her voice in the wind
instructing me
lovingly.

The Pilot

He's spent decades
preparing for this job,
has put in hours of practice with different aircrafts;
from passenger planes to helicopters to commercial,
there's nothing his steady hands and gentle spirit
can't handle.

In the same way he handles a plane in the skies,
he guides his family through turbulence;
with a quiet confidence
and the sun's sparkle in his eyes.
He's piloted them through trouble and saved the day
more times than they can ever count
and in more ways than they can ever know.

He elevates his family to heights they never knew were
possible,
points them in the right direction and shows them how
to use the compass
so they can always find their way.
The sky is the limit if they can only read it,
and he teaches them to make sense of this bird's eye
view.
He guides them through maps in the clouds

and tells them when it's okay to just observe with
wonder
the world below.

Without their faithful and trusted pilot,
his family would be lost and at danger of crashing.
They look to him for his strength and guidance
and in these moments of grounded learning,
they can still see the way the sun sparkles in his eyes,
can still see that he holds the spirit
of the sky.

Cigarettes on the Table

The door squeaks open
and sunlight creeps in
as I bound into your arms,
overjoyed by seeing you
so soon.
Your strong, suntanned arms hold me close
while I inhale
the earthy, nicotinic comfort
you exude.
Hands blackened by oil
gently set me down
as you stretch your legs
so that your cracked lips
can gently press a passing kiss
to the top of my head.
Your thick, crass, country slur
lumbers through an apology
about misplacing your favorite jacket,
the one that hangs loosely on your broad shoulders.
Squatting,
you carelessly rummage
through that cardboard box of clothing
still waiting to go home with you.
Having found

that weather-worn cracked leather,
you exit with a sure stride
and playfully wink
a promise
that you'll be back soon.

But I know
years will pass
before you come back
in search of that tattered blue flannel
I found at the bottom of the box
and claimed as my own personal reminder
that you're real.

Favorite Aunt

She has always clung to each of my thoughts;
from as small as I can remember to now
my words have mattered to her.
She listened to every story I ever told
with rapt attention,
no matter if it was my first time telling it
or my ten thousandth.
She has always treated each word I say the same way she
continues to treat me—
specially.

We used to have sleepovers,
and she would let me stay up late watching my favorite
movies
while also finding time to show me her favorites of all-
time;
she exposed me to such a rich cinematic history
that others talk about as groundbreaking,
but I can only talk about
as hers.
She gave me freedom of self-expression;
let me draw magnet-framed masterpieces for her fridge
and would play whatever I wanted,
whether it was a make-believe game

or one with a board.
She encouraged my dreams,
would read every short story I ever wrote
and kept these scraps of paper
that I can't even remember writing
for years.

She knows every dream and goal I've ever had,
can tell me stories about me that only she knows
because even I
have forgotten them.
She can tell you what my favorite color was at every age,
the grade I made in 8th grade geometry,
and who I had a crush on at 13
because everything about me
was just that important
to her.

She was always there,
cheering me on from the sidelines,
taking me to lunch and chatting about life,
a constant source of brightness and positivity for me.
And she is also a lovely, magical blueprint for me;
she has taught me everything I need to know
about being an aunt,
and because of her I can now fill her shoes

and be the favorite aunt
for my own niece.

Ringmaster

We declared ourselves best friends forever,
you,
me,
and K----
but you never really quite saw us
as friends.

You were more like a ringmaster,
selecting us as acts
to audition for your circus
based on our vulnerability
and being elementary school outcasts
desperate for any type of belonging.
You gave us tents with our names on them,
made us feel special by having this space all our own
and a guaranteed spot in your show;
but each week the auditions started anew,
and we never truly knew
what you expected from our performances
so we always doubted
if we'd be chosen as your weekly headliner.
K---- and I were never truly your friends,
just puppets with starring roles
in your twisted marionette side-show.

We left your circus as we changed schools
with promises of forever from each of us.
You must have found new performers,
because after all these years
"best friends forever" is only true
because it doesn't include
you.

Angel

He paces the middle school hallways with unmatched
carelessness
and the popular kid army at his side.
It's obvious to everyone
that he knows he has it all—
the hair, the style, the attitude, the status, the friends.
All the guys want to be his friend
and all the girls want to date him
because he's the perfect balance
of good and bad—
he makes decent grades, but isn't too smart;
he's not a trouble-maker
but always checks his phone between classes;
he keeps a small group of friends,
but still manages to stay the most popular.
He's a trend-setter,
keeps a close eye on how to stay cool
and brings new habits and practices to the school.
He runs the eighth grade so well
you could almost forget he only just transferred in this
year.
But that was part of his appeal,
the way he picked up on all of our old habits—
like sticking pieces of paper into girls frizzy, curly hair

to see who could stick in the most before these girls
noticed—
and paid no heed to the hearts he broke
when he'd ask out the nerdy, awkward, unpopular girls
as a joke.

His legend lives on in that school forever,
the memories and feelings of his reign embedded
in the institutionally white bricks
which now hold the weight of the pain he caused to
others
just so he
could fit in.

The Big Bad Wolf

Once upon a time there was a girl
who really didn't know much about the world
and she was raised to see the best in everyone.
When she got into high school and was ready to start
dating,
the only protection she had built around her heart
was a straw shanty.

One day a big bad wolf was strolling around the school
and he saw this young girl,
saw the fragile walls she had built
and thought it might be quite nice
to blow down the walls she called home
so that she would take refuge in him
and he could control her.

He walked up to her one day
and started innocent conversations.
When she tried to let her own insecurities close the door
on this potential relationship,
he filled his lungs with false compliments and love
bombing,
huffing and puffing until the straw walls
blew away in the gusts of wind he created.

But before he could fully destroy her,
could exercise complete control,
she caught on to his pathological lies
and ran away for a time
to build up better walls—
weather-worn logs stacked hastily
in a semblance of safety.

Her friends had seen the progress she made,
felt proud of her work and confident in her.
They bolstered her defenses with encouragement and
kindness
until she had developed a new sense of security
and control.
The big bad wolf still had a place in her heart, though,
and she wished so much for it to become a happy
relationship
that she let him come back to the door,
gave him another chance
to get in.

But it didn't take long for the big bad wolf to notice
that the new defenses were stronger than his old tactics
and that he'd have to adapt.
Each day he schemed new ways to tear down the new
walls.

He tried to disarm her by offering her praise for her new
cabin
in the form of gas lighting
and worked his way in little by little.
With the new gas lighting installed,
the big bad wolf huffed and puffed—
said he'd kill himself without her
and set the flame ablaze from within,
burning the log house
down to the ground.

The girl wasn't ready to give in yet,
didn't want to surrender to the wolf's every whim
so she ran to her friends for help.
Together they built a new fortress,
her friends supplying the bricks and mortar
and helping her lay each brick securely,
building her up even faster
than he could tear her down.
When she finally felt safe with her knights all around
her
she ended the relationship,
told the wolf it was over between them.

But the wolf wasn't ready for that;
he huffed and puffed his lies
but they couldn't blow down the house.

He huffed and puffed his threats
but she had taken out the gas lighting.
He huffed and puffed until he was out of breath
and he stepped away for a time to think.
The girl sighed with relief, thinking she was free
and while she rested he built a ladder of rumors
to get to the roof so he could try to slide down the
chimney.
Luckily one of her friends noticed,
dismantled the ladder rung by rung as she dispelled the
rumors
and nearly caught the wolf in the process,
maiming his tail
as he ran away.

The girl survived with her brick-walled heart intact,
never to hear from or see the wolf again.
And legend has it that the big bad wolf is still prowling
for another girl with fragile defenses
but the sight of his scarred tail serves as a red flag of
warning
and he can't ever seem to make it
to their doors.

First Love

They say teenage love isn't meant to last,
that it's all romanticized ideas and puppy-love,
so maybe we read the writing on the chalkboard
and decided independently
not to try for something
we could never keep.

But even though we never tried,
never dared breathe a word the feelings we were
developing until it was too late,
we kept finding ourselves right at the precipice
of a decision that we both ran from.

When we first met it wasn't like this,
wasn't something deep and complex and scary.
It was world history and it felt
like we were from different worlds.
You were an athlete,
seemed so arrogantly full of yourself
even though you had nothing to offer
outside of your looks.
And I was the nerdy honor-student,
too awkward and naïve for a real relationship
and too innocent

to be any fun.
That semester was spent bickering,
a slow process of us learning about each other
while pretending we weren't invested in this friendship
especially since we couldn't know
if our paths would ever cross again.

But then there was pre-AP English,
and you always made sure to sit by me.
We got to know each other without hiding our
friendship,
and I got to see past the mask you wore each day;
I saw you for your quiet brilliance,
got to know what you liked and disliked,
learned your gentle kindness and your true intentions.

I heard what people said, of course—
that I carried you academically
(even though you always kept pace with me)
and that I could never land someone like you,
someone so far out of my league and above my social
status.
All of my friends thought you were annoying,
told me all the reasons you weren't good for me
and I swore you were just
a friend.
In an effort to show that I didn't like you like that

and to convince myself the same,
I helped you connect with other girls
and deepen relationships with anyone but me.

Despite all this, it wasn't love at first sight,
but it was chemistry
sophomore year, pre-AP,
when I fell so hard, so fast,
so hopelessly for you.
From our labs to group work to lecture,
you were always there sitting beside or behind me
and I knew I couldn't help how I felt anymore.
But each time I felt my feet falling out from beneath me,
found myself at the edge of confessing my feelings,
I ran.
And you did the same
until circumstance pushed us apart
and there was nothing to lose by admitting how you felt;
our friendship and memories would forever be intact,
no messy breakups or falling out of favor with the other.

You were moving back to Texas,
I was starting a new school.
We said goodbye in person, and then you sent me a
message
admitting I hadn't imagined the unfolding love story
between us

and that moment
is forever burned in my mind
along with your reaction
when I told you the truth, too;
that I'd felt the same way
for a year.

We convinced ourselves it was okay
to never have given this relationship a chance,
that we didn't lose anything
because we never would have lasted anyway;
we let our communication fizzle into nothingness,
knowing the same exact thing would have happened
to such a fragile, young relationship.

What a bittersweet heartbreak that was
to have and to lose my first love
in the same day.

Modest Woman

Modesty:
A behavior, manner, or *appearance*
intended to avoid impropriety
or indecency.

She stands at the front of the repurposed classroom,
clothed in an ankle length skirt,
a shirt with a high neckline
and sleeves that completely cover her shoulders,
reciting this definition to a room full of teenaged girls.
She quotes Bible verses at them
about clothing themselves with strength and dignity,
stating her imagined dress code time and time again,
never missing a chance to impart her own wisdom and
grace
to the girls two generations beneath her.
She behaves as if the way they dress
influences their chances of salvation.
She speaks and acts in a way that suggests
there's a magic, predetermined length for their hem lines
and sleeves
that will make them worthy of entry into the kingdom,
will make them
modest.

And when these girls do not measure up to these unwritten,
predestined standards,
she requests them to leave,
change their clothing and then return.
It has become second nature for her to daily shame these girls
in the name of love;
she believes this helps instruct them in Godly living
and is blind to all of the ways that it makes them grow distant
from the church and their faith.

She takes time to reinforce these ideals
by placing the behavior of teenaged boys
into the hands of these shamed teenage girls
with anecdotes about the effects their clothing choices
have on the young men in the congregation
and highlights the importance of this
by making it clear that these effects of immodest dress
are beyond their teenaged comprehension.
These girls receive constant messaging from her
that they aren't good enough,
aren't smart enough,
aren't modest enough to participate.

And throughout all her talk of modesty,
of which she herself stated includes behaviors, manners,
and appearances
she only ever preaches on appearances.
She never talks of modest behaviors,
likely because it may highlight all of the ways
in which her teachings on modest appearances
have been immodest.

How exhausted she must be
by spending so much time touting these ideals and views
yet still managing to fall short herself.

The Chameleon

We all have auras,
colors distinctly our own
that help us stand out and apart
and know the truest things we can ever know
about each other.
We call our auras our true colors;
we can mask them,
we can hide them,
but we can never change them.

I try to hide my colors
when I first meet someone new,
try to throw blankets of armor around me
in case people don't like what they see,
in case they don't want to know
the real me.
And you do the same thing,
use coverings to hide your truest self
so when we first met
neither of us saw past the surface
to the colors underneath.
But with time and trust my blankets fell
and I slowly chinked through your armor
until we both found in each other

a best friend.

I loved your pastel hues
of light-hearted fun;
loved the way your good but broken family,
your anxiety and insecurities
shaded in the blank spots,
added a richness and complexity.
Your aura seemed so distinctive, so pure
and you accepted me fully and whole-heartedly
for all the colors I have
and those I lack.

As the years passed our friend groups intersected and
overlapped,
our circle widening, but I wasn't worried
since I thought I could always spot your aura
in a crowd.

But then something strange happened one day
when you didn't plan on seeing me
and our paths crossed anyway.
I saw your face,
but not your shine;
in passing you blended in with everyone else
and you wouldn't meet my eye.
I watched you more in times like these;

watched, mesmerized,
as the pastel hues I thought were yours
shifted to vibrant neon's,
somber greyscales,
colors changing and clashing in the haze of transition
as you went from friend to friend.
Whatever you saw in others,
you made your own
and I had to come to terms with knowing
I never really knew you.

You navigate this world
with your armor glued to your body,
shifting and changing who you are each moment
like a chameleon who's only safety
is to just blend in;
but even chameleon's have true colors
and I never got a chance to see yours
because you never let me in.

"Guys Girl"

She fills her social media
with posts about finding love
and what it means to be a true friend;
she floods her page with photos of her dog
and statuses and photos that celebrate her friends and
family
for the whole world to see.
If all you knew of her was this collection of pictures and
words,
you'd be surprised to see
the way she scoffs at girls' nights,
at the idea of nights spent at the bar
drinking with the girls that will one day be her
bridesmaids
and dancing until their feet hurt,
or of days spent at the spa
with the only aim to relax and talk about their crushes,
their hopes, and their dreams.
You'd be shocked to hear her talk
about how dumb all these things are,
how unnecessary she finds the girls that thrive on this
togetherness
and how she doesn't have time
for all that drama.

If you looked for her true feelings within her online
presence,
you'd likely see posts from the salon,
showing her newly done nails and her freshly dyed hair
with some caption about how special her guy best friend
that went with her is.
She takes pride in being
"not like the other girls",
hides behind this aura of individuality
and protects herself from sisterhood
by disparaging women publicly
and inflating the egos of men.

Maybe one day she'll wake up and see
that the only thing separating her from being like the
other girls
is her own
insecurity.

We Can't Remain Unsaid

Stumbling through countless unsatisfactory lovers,
I can't stop thinking of how they aren't you.
You, my precious doll with the sweetest
round eyes and guileless smile.
Our relationship was my favorite secret,
but how could it not be?

I remember it fondly, Bea:
when we first became lovers,
you insisted on secrecy
and I solemnly agreed for you.
I can still picture your subtle smiles
before you glued your mouth to mine, kissed me sweetly.

I'll always cherish our moments together for the
sweetness
they carry: like the time we were chased by bees,
and I couldn't breathe; I was hunched over, panting,
smiling
because your braying laughter was full of love.
I wanted to tell everyone about you,
about us, but we were meant to stay secret.

This was my most painful secret

because it's hard not to share something so candy-sweet.
When others asked about you,
it was always *here's my friend Bea*
and nothing of our behind-closed-doors lovership,
nothing but cordial smiles.

And yet these thoughts still make me smile.
Every part of our secretive
time together as fervid lovers
is a collection of memories so bittersweet.
I couldn't keep us private, so we weren't meant to be.
There was no compromise; just me, lost without you.

And yet I still exalt you
for your warm, crooked-toothed smile.
And now it's impossible for our past to be
a shadow, a memory, or a secret
anymore— because you painted gently, sweetly
on my heart with your pure love.

So I'll always think of you as my darling Beasley,
the sweet melody of a girl with a pinched smile
who secretly changed my world when she took me as a
lover.

Vidalia Onions

It's the second time I've met his family,
crowded into the small kitchen around the table
with his parents, sister, and little brother.
The kitchen wallpaper is a cigarette-tinged grape print
and the worn wooden table that barely fits in the kitchen
barely seats the six of us.
They've cooked burgers and baked beans,
set out on whatever counterspace they could find
with onions, tomatoes, lettuce, pickles, and sauces
crammed into the empty spaces.

His little brother complains about the onions,
says the smell is overpowering and gross
as if the permanent cigarette stench could possibly be
overpowered
by one onion.
His dad laughs,
picks up an onion slice whole and tells him,
"These ones are sweet,
just try it"
before eating it plain
to prove his point.

His little brother obliges,

selects the smallest sliver he can find
and nibbles off the end of it.
As he chews this tiny morsel,
his eyes, nose, and mouth
all scrunch in response.
"He hates it",
he announces to the room with a laugh.

In that moment I was struck
by how easily he could read disgust on his little brother's
face
when he could never read it
on mine.

Explorer

Nothing about us made sense;
I was shy and quiet,
guarding pieces of myself,
trying to be nothing more than good enough
and you saw me
as a mystery to unravel.
You were chaos and freedom,
asking life for more,
bearing your soul to the world
like fireworks in the night that captivated me.
Before we came upon one another,
we were just strangers
wandering off the beaten paths
looking for something bigger than ourselves.
When our rambling expeditions intersected,
it felt like we had been magnetically drawn to one
another,
such an unexpected happenstance
that it felt like it could have only
been fate.

I cautiously accepted your company on this journey,
let you shelter me at night and envelope me in safety.
I kept my guard up as long as I could,

resisting your daily efforts to break down my defenses.
Small actions made small breaks in the walls I had built,
and I could feel them slowly falling around me.
When my guard had taken almost all the battering it
could,
I made the conscious decision
to tear down the rest of it
for you
just to find you gone from our stronghold the next
morning.
I frantically searched for you,
yelled your name into the trees until my throat was raw
and heard nothing in return,
never saw a sign that you would come back for me.
Through the tears bursting from deep within me,
I barely managed to glimpse
the path you blazed without me,
and I couldn't help
but second guess everything.

I lied to myself,
made myself believe you did this for us,
that you wanted me to be more and do more
now that I wasn't a mystery.
So I followed you through this trail,
searched for you for days
until you circled back for me.

I let you act as if nothing had happened,
let you pretend you had never left me
as you led me deeper and deeper into this unmapped
jungle.
My mind fought a war with my heart as we journeyed;
my mind said this couldn't be healthy,
that someone who can leave me like that
can't actually be my safety.
But my heart thrived on the adventure,
wanted me to let every moment be magic and revelry,
to see the journey as new and exciting—
until the story repeated itself again.

But each time you'd leave,
you left me breadcrumbs that my heart turned into proof
that you cared about me.
I'd nourish myself on these pieces of your soul,
follow the trail until we met again,
because I knew you'd always come back for me
if I just kept following.
And one day we finally found the end of the trail,
stood hand in hand at the edge of a cliff
with each of the previous battles behind us
and I looked to you with hopeful eyes—
hopeful that this would be the end of being left behind—
and you
threw me over the edge,

left me splayed out beneath you in that seemingly
bottomless cavern
as a safety net.

While I clung to my fragile hold,
you went on new adventures;
you found new people,
other lost souls like mine
that you could lead and leave and some of them
even hurt you.
But you knew right where you left me,
and anytime these new people failed you,
you came back to me.
You threw yourself into me,
knowing I would catch and comfort you.
You'd rest in my safety and comfort,
lick your wounds until you were able to chisel steps in
the cliff-face
to free yourself from this desolate place.
Yet you never reached down for me,
never offered me the stability I'd need
to climb up those steps you created.

You'd repeat this cycle time and time again,
bringing me stories of the world I was missing
and praising my strength and loyalty
to keep me hanging there.

Each time you came back I let you crash into me,
let you wear down my strength as I held us both up
foolishly believing
that I needed you to bolster me,
that if I held on for long enough
you'd finally come back for good,
would pull me out of this cavern
and keep me from hurting.

But one day I lost my faith in you;
I knew without your help to leave this abyss,
all I could do was let go and hope the fall wouldn't kill
me
so I did.
The fall wasn't what you said it would be.
The fall hurt less
than each time you fell into me.
I just hope next time you need safety,
need someone to catch you when you fall,
you don't crash headfirst
into these desolate walls.

Ice Queen

You are a sculptor;
your words,
the chisel.
You've used your tools to construct an ice castle
from which you can rule
over this kingdom of your own creation.
You've taken time
to select your royal court;
you've armed knights with your broken philosophies,
sharpened each sword with your misconceptions
and convinced them they are upholding a just cause
by upholding your rule.

You've enslaved the local peasants,
pitted them against each other and created so much in-
fighting
they don't even notice the complete mastery you've
achieved
over this invisible province
and how you've relegated and redefined roles
to fit your own narrative.

Your palace has become so strong, so imminent
that the ground freezes beneath your every step

as your empire expands into new realms.
Your knights take in new prisoners as quickly as you
make new enemies
and make you feel
invincible.

But you've crossed into a new threshold;
where you thought you'd find new thralls,
you found the peasants
that rebel.
These peasants won't go down without a fight;
they carry flames at their sides
and crave the warmth your domain suffocates.
Your fiefdom can only survive
when everything is as cold as you
and their souls are ablaze;
their mere proximity melts the land around you,
reclaiming territories once thought lost
and eventually
they will burn your fortress
to the ground.

Superheroes

A hero
is an ordinary person.
And nothing can make you feel more ordinary
than being a teenage girl
who just
started high school.

A hero
faces overwhelming obstacles.
Like being sexually abused
by your godfather
who has offered your family financial and emotional
support
for as long as you can remember
and teaches Sunday school
at your church.

Heroes find strength.
And nothing can be stronger
than finding your voice
and speaking your truth.
Nothing
is braver than fighting for justice
for yourself,

for your cousin,
and for those who have yet
to find their voice.

Heroes persevere
and endure.
But to endure the criminal justice system
as a teen,
to persevere
through a police investigation
and a prosecution
goes far beyond
heroic.

A superhero
is someone with extraordinary power.
The kind of extraordinary
that is facing your rapist in court,
never wavering from your truth
and being able to win the case
with a plea
of guilty.

A---- and M----
you
are my superheroes.

You

As I feel the gentle heat of your body
seeping into my own
and your weight pressed against me
as I drift into sleep, I can't help but wonder
when it happened--
when did my heart leave my body
and attach itself to you?

When did you become the carrier of my heart,
an extension of me
roaming the world?
Did you know it would create this pull,
cause me to only ever feel whole
when we are together?
Did you know *you*
would redefine the meaning of the word home,
would make it so that home
could only ever mean
you?

How could anyone know this feeling--
the feeling of wearing your heart
on someone else's sleeve--
well enough to put it into words?

How could anyone know what it is to love so completely,
know something this painfully pure,
when they don't have you?

There will never be
another you;
never be another vessel
to carry my heart around this world
the same way you do.
You are forever entrusted with this burden of my love,
and I will aim to repay you for this blessing,
this service,
until the end of my days.

The Muse

As I feel the gentle heat of your body
seeping into my own
and your weight pressed against me
as I drift into sleep, I can't help but wonder
when it happened--
when did my heart leave my body
and attach itself to you?

When did you become the carrier of my heart,
an extension of me
roaming the world?
Did you know it would create this pull,
cause me to only ever feel whole
when we are together?
Did you know *you*
would redefine the meaning of the word home,
would make it so that home
could only ever mean
you?

How could anyone know this feeling--
the feeling of wearing your heart
on someone else's sleeve--
well enough to put it into words?

How could anyone know what it is to love so completely,
know something this painfully pure,
when they don't have you?

There will never be
another you;
never be another vessel
to carry my heart around this world
the same way you do.
You are forever entrusted with this burden of my love,
and I will aim to repay you for this blessing,
this service,
until the end of my days.

The Expert

She's the one with the specialized skills,
the knowledge,
the fancy degree framed on her wall
declaring her to have some level of mastery in her field
and showing everyone who enters her office
how important she is.
She has the years of experience
that make her the knower of all things,
the time and research that has honed her intuition
so that she knows her employees well,
knows how to talk to them and interact in ways
they'll be receptive to.
In fact, she gets it right so often
she's started to abandon her curiosity;
she has a full toolbelt at her disposal
she's stopped reaching for,
stopped using to find the clues she relied on
to help her always get it right.

Does she ever really know
anymore
if she's truly gotten it right,
or if she just thinks she has?

Too Much

She lights up every room she enters;
has a unique and joyful look that turns heads.
Everyone wants to bask in her beauty, her youth, her
pure delight
at life.
She is young and exuberant,
but she also has a quiet elegance;
a way of sitting with her head held high
that could almost suggest nobility
even though no one would be able to know her history
just from looking at her.

She tends to be gentle and sweet;
she divides her attention so that everyone can have a
piece,
everyone can have that time they crave
with her.
And she is so eager to please,
thrives on adoration and kind words,
that she has practiced her actions carefully
to craft this image that makes people love her.
She doesn't want anyone to see through this charade
and see her fears and her reality,
see how little control

she truly has.

She's terrified of the unfamiliar;
when confronted with her worst fears
she reacts loudly and out of character.
She may flee dramatically,
or loudly voice her feelings in a way
she will later be ashamed of.
She relies so heavily on those she loves to keep her safe
that after she's reacted
she needs them to talk her down from the ledge
because she has a death grip on her adoration.
When her disruptions happen,
her desire to revert to how it was before
may come off as abrasive
and can make people say all the things about herself
she's so tired of hearing
as her personality continues to rack up the same old
tired complaints:
She's too loud
too annoying
too needy
too much.

But she knows at home she can rest soundly
in the solitude of those who love her so completely.
She feels her truest self with these people

and she loves them for loving every part of her—
for seeing her brilliance and not faulting her when it
fails,
for knowing her every want without her having to
vocalize it,
for making her feel safe and free to express herself,
for helping her to be the best possible version of herself
with gentle corrections
and constant adoration of every one of her
imperfections.
They never make her feel like everyone else does
when these cracks let her truest self shine through;
they let her be soft when the world says she is hard,
let her feel safe enough to assert her needs
no matter how small or insignificant they may seem.
They love her wholeheartedly,
love her for all her perfect imperfections
and embody the fact that she will never be too much
because she will always be just enough
for those that matter.

The Singer

She is an artist,
sharing pieces of her soul with the world
through her songs.
And through this generous offering she's given us,
she helped raise and define me,
kept me grounded
in truth and authenticity.
Regardless of our differences,
both in personality and lived experiences,
her music has always been able to offer me
comfort, safety, and understanding.

Laced into her melodies are beautifully crafted lessons,
things she's been able to teach me throughout my life—
like the importance of fighting for myself,
of never settling for less than I deserve
and that every fairytale ending
isn't always quite what it seems.
She taught me that my voice has power,
that I should speak my truth
and the world will hear me.

She showed me how vulnerability can be powerful,
that it's a piece of the prism within me,

a reflection of the beautiful colors that run through my
veins.
And she masterfully displayed the power of words,
how they can both hurt and heal;
she taught me to be okay
with knowing the only words I can control
are my own.

She showed me how to love every part of myself
and how to stay true to me
so that I would never lose my individuality
in pursuit of someone else.
And she reminded me to never take myself so seriously
that I can't laugh at my own mistakes
and learn from them.

She told me to be brave, to be me;
showed me that the courageous act is the most
important thing.
She sang songs of our history,
taught me to learn from those who came before me
and that there can always be beauty
underneath the tragedy.

She told me there is enough love in this world
for all of us,
told me to ask for more

so that I could love more,
love deeper,
love fearlessly.
She told me to be open to the world,
and it would open itself to me.

She taught me lessons beyond the depth of her music;
she taught me how to be so creatively me
that I could put words on a page and create a
masterpiece
if I only could take the time to believe
in the possibility.